Green Mt Ranger.

Cornerstones of Freedom

The Story of DISCARD

THE GREEN MOUNTAIN BOYS

By Susan Clinton

CHILDRENS PRESS ®

CHICAGO

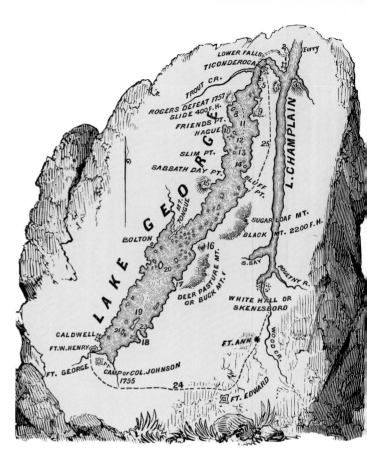

Ticonderoga (above) and a map of the country around the fort (right). Cannon atop the southern wall of the fort (below right) guarded the channel between Lake George and Lake Champlain.

Library of Congress Cataloging-in-Publication Data

Clinton, Susan.
    The story of the Green Mountain Boys/by Susan Clinton.
        p.   cm. — (Cornerstones of freedom)
    Summary: Discusses the activities of the Green Mountain Boys under the leadership of Ethan Allen, first working as a private part-time army to defend land ownership rights in the colony which later became Vermont, and then fighting in the Revolutionary War in various areas in the northern colonies.
    ISBN 0-516-04731-0
    1.   Allen, Ethan, 1738-1789—Juvenile literature.   2.   Vermont-History—Revolution, 1775-1783—Campaigns—Juvenile literature.   3.   New York (State)—History—Revolution, 1775-1783—Campaigns—Juvenile literature.   4.   Ticonderoga (N.Y.)—History—Revolution, 1775-1783—Juvenile literature.   5.   United States—History—Revolution, 1775-1783—Campaigns—Juvenile literature.   [1.   Vermont—History—To 1791.   2.   United States—History—Revolution, 1775-1783—Campaigns.   3.   Allen, Ethan, 1738-1789.   I.   Title.   II.   Series.
E207.A4C44 1987   87-17380
973.3—dc19   CIP
                                                              AC

Childrens Press, Chicago
Copyright ©1987 by Regensteiner Publishing Enterprises, Inc.
All rights reserved. Published simultaneously in Canada.
Printed in the United States of America.
1 2 3 4 5 6 7 8 9 10 R 96 95 94 93 92 91 90 89 88 87

At 4:00 A.M. on May 10, 1775, Captain Delaplace and most of the fifty British soldiers inside Fort Ticonderoga were sleeping soundly. Only a few guards stood watch over one of the most important British forts in the American colonies. From its tall, wood and stone walls, cannons aimed down through the darkness at Lake Champlain.

Lake Champlain is a long lake. It needles its way over one hundred miles from Canada south into New York. At Ticonderoga, the lake is only a mile wide. From this narrow passage, the British fort could control all water traffic between the St. Lawrence River and the rich Hudson Valley. Any boat moving north or south would have to pass under Ticonderoga's guns. If the American colonies were ever foolish enough to rebel against Great Britain, it would be easy for the British to move troops and supplies into battle against them.

So, the British soldiers slept easily behind their walls. It's true the walls were a little crumbly here and there. But summer was coming—Captain Delaplace was already at work on his vegetable garden—there would be plenty of time to mend the defenses and lay in ammunition. Supplies and news reached this remote fort slowly—so slowly that no

Ticonderoga 12th May 1775

Honble Sir, I make You a Present of a Major a Captain and Two Lieuts in the regular Establishment of George the Third I hope they may serve as ransom for some of our Friends at Boston and particularly for Capt Brown of Rhode Island a Party of men under the Command of Capt Herick has Took Possession Scanesborough Imprisoned Major Sceen and Seized a Schooner of his, I Expect in Ten days Time to have it rigged and mand and armed with 6 or 8 Pieces of Canon which with the Boats in our Possession I Purpose to make an attack on the armed Sloop of George the Third which is Now Cruising on Lake Champlain and is about Twice as bigg as the Schooner, I Hope in a Short Time to be authorised to acquaint your Hon= =our that Lake Champlain the fortifications thereon are Subjected to the Colonies The Enterprise has been approbated by the [...]

[...] Green Mountain [...] to the Success [...] Lost in the [...] George's Sloop [...] Capt Worner [...] of Crown Point [...] Governor [...] to oppose us & [...] Messieurs Hicock [...] Charge of Condu[...] [...]d These Gentle= [...]us and active in [...] upon Your [...] in a Situation [...] Contiguous to Canada— I Subscribe my Self Your Honours Ever Faithfull most Obedient and Humble Servant
Ethan Allen
at Present Commander of Ticonderoga

Ethan Allen's report to Johathan Trumbull on the capture of Fort Ticonderoga. In it he suggests using British officers captured at Fort Ticonderoga as ransom for fellow patriots being held by the British.

one inside the fort knew that the first shots of the American rebellion had been fired at Lexington three weeks before. Certainly no one inside dreamed that a bunch of untrained, ragtag American farmers calling themselves the Green Mountain Boys were at that moment creeping through a crumbled wall into their mighty fort.

The eighty-three attackers were led by a large man named Ethan Allen. They moved quietly through the fortified wall and then burst through a flimsy inner gate, startling the lone guard posted there. The panicked guard aimed right at Allen and fired but his gun didn't go off. Then he ran for it. The Green Mountain Boys remembered Ethan Allen waving a sword and running up the stairs to the Captain's quarters shouting, "Come out of there, you old rat!" Allen claimed the fort "In the name of the Great Jehovah and the Continental Congress!" Whatever he said, the sight of all the British soldiers half-asleep, half-dressed, and surrounded by musket-toting frontier farmers convinced Captain Delaplace to surrender immediately. The Green Mountain Boys had taken Fort Ticonderoga without firing a single shot.

Their incredible victory was a great help to the American rebels. Ticonderoga's cannons helped George Washington's army force the British out of Boston. For the moment, Ethan Allen and his farmers were heroes. This was a big change for the Green Mountain Boys; many people in the neighboring colony of New York thought of them as a gang of bullies and outlaws. To some extent, the New Yorkers (Yorkers, as the Green Mountain Boys called them) were right. Since 1770, when some angry settlers had banded together and formed the Green Mountain Boys, they had been fighting a land war. Not against the British, but against the colony of New York.

New Hampshire Grants

By 1773 border disputes arose between the colonies of New Hampshire and New York (left). Governor Benning Wentworth (right) was selling grants of land that the Governor of New York claimed belonged to his colony.

The Green Mountain Boys lived west of the Green Mountains in the present-day state of Vermont. The trouble was, back in the 1750s, no one was sure which colony owned the land these settlers bought. Between 1750 and 1764 Benning Wentworth, the royal governor of New Hampshire, made a tidy profit selling land grants to nearly three million acres, despite the fact that the governor of New York claimed this land as part of his territory. In

1764, the king of England declared that the land belonged once and for all to the colony of New York. New York began granting the land to other buyers, but by 1764, several thousand settlers with New Hampshire land grants were already living there. They called their part of the country the Grants, short for New Hampshire Grants.

Most of the settlers were New Englanders, Yankees used to having a say in their government. They didn't particularly want to be part of the New York Colony which was run by a small group of wealthy men. However, they were resigned to accepting Yorker authority. But they weren't resigned to handing over their land to Yorker buyers or to buying their own land all over again, and at a higher price, too! New Hampshire grants originally cost two cents an acre. New York wanted to charge nine cents an acre just to confirm New Hampshire titles! Nine cents an acre doesn't sound like much, and in fact, the land was worth much more than that. (Anyone who paid nine cents an acre for a New York title could turn around and sell the land for between 25 cents and $1.50 an acre.) But many of the Grants settlers didn't want to sell their land, they wanted to live on it. And for one reason or another, most of the Grants landowners simply didn't have any cash.

New Hampshire's low land prices attracted two very different kinds of buyers: poor farmers who could barely afford the land they bought and land speculators who snapped up as much land as they could afford with the idea of selling it at higher prices later. Speculators who spent every penny on land did not have enough left over to pay New York's fees. For example, Ethan Allen himself was a big speculator. By 1775, he, his brothers, Ira, Heman, and Zimri, and his cousin Remember Baker held sixty thousand acres of Vermont wilderness. Their holdings were worth almost three hundred thousand dollars on paper. If their land titles were no good, they would be in debt the rest of their lives.

The plight of the poor farmers was even worse.

These families had put in years of grinding work turning wild land into farms. Usually, the men came first to cut down trees, clear away underbrush, and put up some kind of a house. For example, one settler stood four long, sturdy branches for cornerposts and made walls out of other branches stuck together with mud.

The men then returned to bring their families out, by boat in the warm months and by sled when the rivers were frozen solid. One Vermont settler named Seth Hubbell described harnessing himself to his wagon when one of his two oxen became sick. He had one hundred miles to go. By the time he reached his land, there was four feet of snow on the ground. That first winter, Hubbell traded an animal skin for some wheat and fed his family on moose meat. Settlers like Hubbell bartered for things they needed and relied on fishing and hunting to keep their families alive through years when the harvest was bad. All they had was their land. When Yorker surveyors began measuring their land for new owners, these farmers were angry.

One October morning on the Breakenridge farm near Bennington, the Yorker surveyors came face to face with James Breakenridge and sixty neighbors, muskets in hand. The farmers called this confrontation a "peaceful parley;" the New York governor called it a "disorderly riot." Whichever it was, the surveyors packed up their tools and went home. New York next went to court. They wanted to force Breakenridge and eight other Bennington landowners off their land.

Everyone knew that the court's decision on these nine farms was going to effect all Grants claims. The court cases centered on Bennington because it was the most settled, and therefore the most hotly disputed, area of the Grants. The New Hampshire title holders would have to defend their claims against some of New York's most powerful citizens—the lieutenant-governor, the attorney-general, the judge on the case, and the prosecuting attorney all had New York titles to land in the Grants. New York's court cases made the Grants settlers and the speculators realize that they needed to work together. They hired Ethan Allen to do the legwork on their defense.

Allen was an experienced woodsman and a great talker (he was fluent, vivid, and very, very loud). He had ranged widely over the Grants, visiting with many of the people on it. The first thing people noticed about him was his size; he was a big, powerful man. He had to have been strong to survive some of his ordeals. On one cold, rainy autumn trek, Ethan was caught at sunset far from camp. With his

Ethan Allen

clothes soaked through and starting to freeze on him, he marked off a circle and kept moving. He tramped round and round his path all night long to keep from freezing to death. Tough frontier farmers on the Grants reported that Ethan could bite the heads off nails, or strangle a bear with his bare hands. Even if they're not true, these legends show the admiration the Grants settlers felt for him.

Allen traveled about four hundred miles gathering title documents and hiring a lawyer. As it turned out, none of his efforts made any difference. In the first few minutes of the first trial, the New York judge ruled that the New Hampshire titles were worthless. Allen and the lawyer didn't wait to hear their side lose case after case. Allen packed up his papers and rode back to Bennington. As word of his coming spread, anxious settlers gathered at the Catamount Tavern to hear the verdict.

The Catamount Tavern was a square building sitting on top of a hill with a good view of the Bennington countryside. *Catamount* (cat of the mountain) is another word for the mountain lion that still roamed the Vermont woods in the 1770s. The tavern had a large stuffed catamount standing on a wooden platform at the top of a twenty-foot pole for its sign. It was snarling in the direction of New York.

Allen's description of the trial wasn't calculated

The Old Catamount Tavern (left) in Bennington. Catamount Monument (right)

The Green Mountain Boys in council

to calm the settlers down. In his version, the poor, hardworking, and innocent Grants settlers were being tricked out of their land by a small group of greedy Yorker speculators. This wasn't completely accurate. There were plenty of speculators on the Grants side and many had purchased land knowing full well the titles were risky. However, accurate or not, Allen's report made the settlers angry. They weren't going to pay and they weren't going to leave their land—they were going to fight.

Within a few months, the Grants settlers had organized their own militia. This volunteer, part-time army was made up of farmers who were ready to drop their plows, pick up their muskets, and drive out any Yorkers who dared to claim even an inch of their land. Each settlement had its own company and each company, its own elected captain. Their colonel commandant was Ethan Allen and the Catamount Tavern was their headquarters. They had no uniforms, outside of a sprig of evergreen in their hats; no cannons or even standard muskets. They would not be able to hold off trained, disciplined New York troops, but they were gambling that they wouldn't have to.

One Yorker official wrote, "They assemble themselves together in the night time and throw down all the Yorker fences, etc., and drive the Cattle into the

fields and meadows and destroy both Grass and Corn, and do every mischief they can think of." New York's Governor Colden threatened to chase Allen and his rowdy followers back to the Green Mountains. In answer, the Grants' militia defiantly named themselves the Green Mountain Boys.

Their first targets were the Yorker surveyors. In spring 1771, someone sighted surveyors working about sixty miles north of Bennington. Allen rounded up some men, all disguised with Indian war paint, for the two-day ride, but he didn't want to charge into a fight. Instead he sent one man ahead to warn surveyor William Cockburn that the Green Mountain Boys were coming to murder any surveyors they found. Cockburn didn't wait to meet them; he packed up his tools and rushed back to New York.

Blustering was one of the Green Mountain Boys' best tactics—their bloodcurdling threats probably prevented a lot of real bloodshed. In five years of resistance, the Green Mountain Boys threatened many people and beat up some; they even whipped a few men (as Ira Allen says, "chastised them with the twigs of the forest"), but they didn't kill anyone. A few months later, in the summer of 1771, they were surprised to find how far organized blustering would carry them.

That summer, the high sheriff of Albany County, Henry Ten Eyck, gathered a posse of about one hundred fifty Yorker farmers and set out on the thirty-mile march to Bennington. Ten Eyck's goal was to evict James Breakenridge once and for all. After a two day march the sheriff and his men could see the farm, across a little bridge half a mile away. The farmhouse itself bristled with musket bores — about twenty friends of Breakenridge had locked themselves inside and cut loopholes in the walls for their guns. In a field on one side of the house were about forty more settlers with their guns ready. As Ten Eyck marched resolutely forward, he spotted another big cluster of muskets behind a ridge on the other side of the house. He was marching into a funnel of Green Mountain muskets.

When they saw the guns, the sheriff's reluctant posse began to slip away. By the time Ten Eyck got to the farmhouse door, he had around twenty men instead of one hundred fifty. The frustrated sheriff yelled that he would break down the door. As soon as he said it, several hundred rifles aimed right at him. The sheriff gave up; and with the few men left in his posse marched away leaving the Green Mountain Boys to celebrate their victory.

The Green Mountain Boys didn't stop at defending their land. They ran off anybody who dared to

Allen forcing New York settlers off their land

stake out a Yorker land grant, even if the settlers were themselves poor farmers who knew nothing about the land dispute. For example, one group of Scotch families, newly arrived in the colonies, started clearing farms near New Haven. Just as their first harvest drew near, a band of one hundred Green Mountain Boys attacked. While their horses trampled and ate the crops in the field, the Boys burned cabins and haystacks, wrecked the flour mill and smashed the millstones, and threatened to skin the surprised and terrified settlers alive. Of course, no one was actually skinned alive; instead, the Scots were given just enough food for the trip back to New York and sent away to tell their tale.

The Green Mountain Boys attacked a group settled near Rupert in 1771. For this, New York ordered the arrest of the "abominable wretches, rioters, and traitors," and offered a reward for the capture of Ethan Allen, his cousin Remember Baker, and seven others. Ethan Allen commented, "By Virtue of a late Law in the Province they are Not Allowed to hang any man before they have ketched him."

One winter night in 1772, a frustrated New York justice of the peace named John Munro decided that he would catch somebody. After dark, he and his men broke into the cabin of Remember Baker. Baker immediately grabbed an ax, chopped a hole in the roof, scrambled out, and jumped right into a snowdrift, where he was captured. In the struggle, one of Munro's men cut off Baker's thumb with his sword. The Yorkers tied up the wounded Baker, threw him in a sleigh, and headed for New York as fast as they could go. Meanwhile, Baker's wife roused the neighbors and a dozen men went riding pell-mell after the Yorkers.

The chase lasted a good part of the night, but in the end, Munro was caught. Baker was carried back to Catamount Tavern to warm up and recover from

Governor Tryon quieting angry settlers

his wound. Released unharmed, Munro continued to live on the Grants and to put up with a great deal of harassment from his Yankee neighbors. Ethan Allen called the attempted capture "a wicked, inhuman, most barbarous, infamous, cruel, villainous, and thievish attack." Munro wrote that the Yankees on the Grants "are possessed with a spirit of contradiction."

The exasperated Governor Tryon of New York hit upon a simple way to attack the Grants resistance— he cut New York's land fees in half. At seven dollars for one hundred acres, new settlers still couldn't afford it—but the more established farmers were tempted. The leaders of The Green Mountain Boys now had to keep the Grants settlers united against New York even if it meant intimidating and silencing them. One dissenting settler, Dr. Samuel Adams, was a Yorker who had moved to Arlington before all the trouble started. When the Green Mountain Boys warned him to stop spreading pro-Yorker arguments, Adams didn't back down. Instead he started carrying two pistols with him everywhere, announcing that he was ready to shoot a hole through anybody who bothered him. One day some Green Mountain Boys dragged Adams off to the Catamount for a makeshift trial. He quickly was found guilty of being a public nuisance. For his punishment, Adams was tied to a chair, then hoisted twenty feet up, to a highly visible seat beside the tavern's stuffed catamount. Two hours later, Adams came down a quieter man.

Throughout the Grants, New York officials found it more and more difficult to do their jobs. In 1773, the New York justice in Clarendon, Benjamin Spencer, was put on trial by the Green Mountain Boys and found guilty of being too loyal to New York. Ethan Allen and his fellow judges, Seth Warner, Remember Baker, and Robert Cochran, wanted Spencer to resign his post. They burned the roof off Spencer's cabin to show they were serious about it. Spencer resigned. The next justice for Clarendon, Benjamin Hough, did not get away so easily. He was sentenced to two hundred lashes and thrown off the Grants altogether.

In 1774, the angry New York Assembly passed a severe law against a whole list of offenses. The penalty for typical Green Mountain Boys' activities, such as interfering with New York officials, burning haystacks, or destroying outhouses, would be death. Ethan Allen immediately named this law the Bloody Act. At a meeting in Manchester, representatives of the Grants settlers passed a resolution forbidding anyone on the Grants to hold any New York office. Without officials, New York would not be able to enforce the Bloody Act—it would not be able to rule the Grants at all. The conflict between the Grants and the colony of New York was beginning to sound like a revolution. As the Grants settlers discussed turning directly to King George III for help against the colony of New York, they were overtaken by the outbreak of the American Revolution.

The Revolution brought a temporary truce between the Grants settlers and the Yorkers. After their victory at Fort Ticonderoga, Ethan Allen and Seth Warner were able to persuade the Continental

Congress, the governing body for the rebelling colonies, that they could make good use of the Green Mountain Boys "in the army to be raised for the defence of America." The Continental Congress didn't have the power to recruit or pay a regiment—that was up to the individual colonies. In this case, it was up to the colony of New York. Armed with the recommendation of the Continental Congress, Allen and Warner went on to New York City. There, even though officially Allen and Warner were still wanted criminals with rewards on their heads, the New York Assembly heard them out and, amazingly, voted to foot the bill for a regiment of five hundred Green Mountain Boys. Moreover, they agreed to provide back pay for all the men who took part in the Ticonderoga attack.

In July 1775, a convention of Grants representatives met to choose officers for their regiment. To Ethan Allen's surprise and disappointment, their choice for commander was the quiet, steady, reliable Seth Warner. When Warner and the Green Mountain Boys moved north with General Montgomery to attack Canada, Ethan Allen came along as a scout. Allen's job was to send back supplies and win over Canadians. After recruiting about eighty Canadian farmers, success convinced Allen that he and his little band, working with another group of Canadian

Allen in prison

recruits under Major John Brown, could take the city of Montreal. The plan failed. Brown never joined the attack and all but thirty-eight of Allen's men deserted. Allen was captured on September 25, 1775, and spent nearly three years as a prisoner of the British. He missed some hard fighting.

On October 30, Warner with a mixed group of Green Mountain Boys and Yorkers kept British reinforcements from crossing the St. Lawrence

River to help defend Montreal. Warner let the boats get close to shore, then ordered his three hundred fifty men to fire. The British had to retreat without landing. The American force took Montreal but failed to take Quebec. The arrival of General John Burgoyne and eight thousand British and German troops ended all American hopes of winning Canada. The Green Mountain Boys brought up the rear as the Americans, suffering from cold, hunger, and an outbreak of smallpox, retreated to Ticonderoga.

Burgoyne drove the Americans out of Ticonderoga on July 6, 1777, and chased them south. Warner and Colonel Turbott Francis with a combined force of nine hundred fifty men held the British back until the Americans were nearly surrounded by German reinforcements. Francis was killed; Warner withdrew, saving only eighty men from his regiment.

The British army was now well into the Grants, scouring the countryside for food and horses. Their years of resisting Yorkers left the Green Mountain Boys and the Grants settlers well prepared for this kind of warfare. The Americans stayed ahead of the British, flooding fields, destroying bridges, cutting down trees for roadblocks, and herding away livestock. Farmers came to the British camp claiming to be on the British side just to steal British muskets and ammunition.

Burgoyne was making such slow progress that he sent out a force of five hundred German dragoons under Colonel Frederich Baum to seize as many horses as they could find in Bennington. When Baum saw a large force coming toward him from Bennington, he told his men to hold their fire—he was expecting pro-British Tories. Instead militiamen from New Hampshire and Vermont stormed over the German troops and scattered them.

Battle of Bennington

As a fresh column of German troops arrived, Warner and his men attacked. They fought the Germans back until it got too dark to fight. The German relief troops left four cannons and hundreds of much needed muskets behind. The Battle of Bennington gave the Americans the edge they needed to defeat Burgoyne and force his surrender in October 1777.

In that same year, a convention of twenty-four delegates voted to declare the Grants a new state, independent of New York. In July 1777, as Burgoyne was advancing against Ticonderoga, a second convention adopted a constitution for the new Republic of Vermont. By the time Ethan Allen

returned to Bennington in May 1778, Vermont had its own elected government.

Ethan Allen took over Vermont's fight for admission to the union. In petition after petition to the Continental Congress, Vermont asked to be admitted as the fourteenth state, even offering to pay a share of the bills for the Revolution. But George Clinton, the powerful governor of New York was able to block Vermont's admission every time. The other members of the Congress were afraid that New York would withdraw its support from the Revolution. In frustration, Allen did a surprising thing—he turned to the British and began secretly negotiating to save Vermont by reuniting it to the British Empire! Allen's arrangements with the British came to nothing, although they did end his long leadership in Vermont.

In 1781, when Seth Warner became too ill to lead the Green Mountain Boys, their regiment was disbanded and sent home. Warner came home wounded and ill with tuberculosis and arthritis. He never fully recovered and died in 1784. Ethan Allen retired to a farm in Burlington, Vermont where he died in 1789 at the ripe old age (for a frontiersman) of fifty. Neither one lived to see Vermont admitted to the United States. New York managed to stall that event for fourteen years. Finally, in 1791, Vermont became the fourteenth state.

Back in 1770, when the Grants settlers first organized themselves into the Green Mountain Boys, they hoped to hold out against New York until King George III could make up his mind about their case. In the end, these "Bennington rioters" full of the "spirit of contradiction" held out long enough to break away from uncongenial rule altogether. Their escapades on the Grants got them into the habit of acting as an independent body; and their sturdy courage in the Continental Army helped break the power of the British in America once and for all.

PICTURE ACKNOWLEDGMENTS

The Bettmann Archives—8, 14, 16, 20, 26
Historical Pictures Service, Chicago—1, 2, 4 (3 photos), 6,
    9 (2 photos), 15 (2 photos), 17, 22, 27, 29, 30
Library of Congress—7
Northwind Picture Archives—11

About the Author

Susan Clinton holds a Ph.D. in English and is a part-time teacher of English Literature at Northwestern University in Chicago. Her articles have appeared in such publications as *Consumer's Digest, Family Style Magazine,* and the Chicago *Reader.* In addition, she has been a contributor to *Encyclopaedia Britannica* and *Compton's* Encyclopedia and has written reader stories and other materials for a number of educational publishers. Her books for Childrens Press include *I Can Be an Architect* and *The Story of Susan B. Anthony.* Ms. Clinton lives in Chicago and is the mother of two boys.